Am I Precious?

Am I Precious?

Belinda McCallion

LANG
BOOK PUBLISHING

langbookpublishing.com

National Library of New Zealand Cataloguing-in-Publication Data

Lang Book Publishing Limited 2014

Edited by Jenny Argante

For more information visit: www.belindamccallion.com/

or join the facebook group: www.facebook.com/bmccallionamiprecious

ISBN-13: 978-0-9941117-7-7

Published in New Zealand

Dedicated to Gianna
and every young girl who needs to know
how precious they are.

I have a secret question
I ask everyone I know.

It's so secret,
people don't even know
I've asked!

I ask my mum

by bringing in the mail for her.

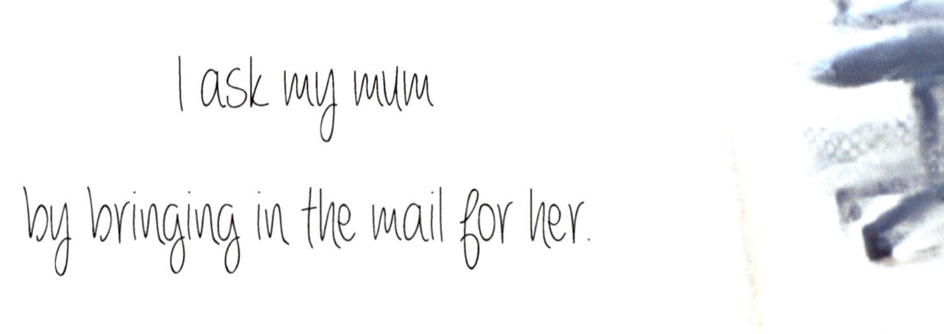

I ask my dad

by making his boring work look beautiful.

I ask my brother

by dressing up his cowboy.

I ask my sister

by showing her how pretty

I can be.

I ask my nana

by picking her the biggest
and best flower.

Entrant No. 18
Tallest
Sunflower
Competition

I ask my granddad

by reading him the longest book
on the shelf.

I ask my friend

by showing her an awesome
spider I found.

6x8 = 49
9x12 = 111
7x6 = 36

I ask my teacher
by doing my work quickly.

I don't always get the answer I want.

So I ask God.
He answers my secret question
with a secret answer.

He whispers it through the cool breeze,
which awakens the flowers to dance,

and He paints it in the sky.

In case I miss it,
He has the heavens shout it,
and the birds sing it.

Even though He answers in different ways,
His answer is always
the same.

"Am I precious?" I ask.

I listen and He answers.

"Yes! You are precious. I made you.

You are my masterpiece.

Look around.

See what I made to remind you
how much I love you and how
precious you are."

Somehow, when God answers,
His answer becomes the most important.

Then when I see someone who needs to know
how precious they are...

I understand.